DOWN AT THE DEEP END

DOWN AT THE DEEP END

poems & drawings

May 10 – August 3, 2012

Daniel Abdal-Hayy Moore

THE ECSTATIC EXCHANGE
2012
Philadelphia

Down at the Deep End
Copyright © 2012 Daniel Abdal-Hayy Moore
All rights reserved.
Printed in the United States of America

For quotes any longer than those for critical articles and reviews, contact:
The Ecstatic Exchange,
6470 Morris Park Road, Philadelphia, PA 19151-2403
email: abdalhayy@danielmoorepoetry.com

First Edition
ISBN: 978-0-578-11367-8 (paper)
Published by The Ecstatic Exchange,
6470 Morris Park Road, Philadelphia, PA 19151-2403

Also available from The Ecstatic Exchange:
Knocking from Inside, poems by Tiel Aisha Ansari

Front cover drawing and back photograph by the author,

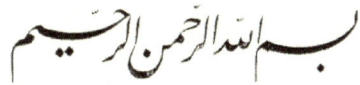

DEDICATION
To
Shaykh ibn al-Habib
(and the continuation of the Habibiyya)
Shaykh Bawa Muhaiyuddeen,
all shuyukh of instruction and ma'arifa,
to
Baji Tayyaba Khanum
of the unsounded depths

and to my wife Malika,
helpmate and solace
in the highest and most
endlessly loving way

to Drs. Ali, DeNittis, Carp, Keane, Fish and Hamid

and all who prayed for my recovery

———

*The earth is not bereft
of Light*

CONTENTS

Author's Introduction   8
God of the Splinter   11
Angelic Shoes   13
Good Cheer Among the Cynics   15
Short Fable of the Three Schooners   17
Seeing the Scaffold   19
All Moving Forward in Time   22
Sweat and Boils   25
Venetian Magicians   27
Prayer   29
Last and First Words   30
My Mother   32
If I Should Die Tonight   36
Poem Begun With a Line by Thomas Tranströmer   39
The Lions' Arena   41
Science Fact Science Fiction   43
I Hear Nearby   44
Poem Ending with Lines by Yeats   47
All's Well   49
Allah   51
The Chemo   52
I Enter a Huge Temple   53
Job Sits in His Chair   56
Falling   58
A Little Blue Monk   60
The Rowers   63
The Soul   67
Small Town   70
The First Two Lines Came During Radiation # 7   72
How Many Sirens More   73
Soul Questions   74
What Fire Prevented   78
Cancer   86

Acceptable   89
Wisdom   91
One Voice Calling Us   93
The Body   94
Leaning My Head on my Hand   100
Dark Chemo Thoughts   103
A Rage of Bravery   105
Only One Thing   106
Newspaper Fantasy   107
Written in Parking Lot after Radiation   109
His Most Precious Concern   111
Ever-Ocean-Flowing Space   113
All Our Attempts at Healing   115
In the Dark Casino   118
The Bloom Upon the Rose   120
Our Hurts   121
On the Sheer Sides of Things   123
Velvets and Icy Metals   125
Young Picadilly People   128
The Finite Sing of the Infinite?   130
Twenty-Eight Poems Ago   133
The Night is a Red Jacket   136
Faithful Slippers   138
Water   140
Back Garden Birdbath   141
Talk   142
Comforting Me   144
High-Flying Wind   146
My Throat   149
Palpable Hugs   150
Phoenix   152
Rainbow Puddles   155
The World   157
Morpho Blue   158
Index   162

AUTHOR'S INTRODUCTION

This may be a secret among only a few of its recipients, but cancer is a direct and positive gift from God. Its chemo and radiation therapies wrack and ruin us, drive us over harsh territories, bring us to the brink, face us with the taste of our mortality even if the cancer itself was unfelt, and its alternative therapies may bewilder us with the arcane and often whacky character of their methods, the dizzying array presented by well-intentioned friends and relatives road-forking us with unthinkable conundrums. I chose the traditional medical program of three chemo and thirty-five radiation sessions, begun immediately after diagnosis of my base-of-tongue cancer, and I praise Allah for the doctors who treated me with their medicine chest of tough love.

It's a shock at first when we find out that something in our bodies, those dear bosom friends of ours, has gone seriously "wrong." Something is out of control, with a will as it were of its own, and could kill us if left to its own devices. You get a sense that as a consciousness and a soul you're situated somewhere outside the main municipal square of the town of your own body, a spectator rather than its lawgiver, and the Lawgiver is really all along and forever God alone. Will you shake your fist from so far away and "fight the disease" which has been so granted to you, or will you work to neutralize its ill effects and make peace with it by your soul's anchoring in holy ground, and praying to that One Alone that your healing method of choice eradicate the disease as efficiently as possible, and as if — why not? — by magic. Cancer can't be left to rampage on its own, dragon-like, licking surrounding cells with its flame. It can't swallow us whole, incinerating us in its bowels.

I entered into negotiations with it with strong faith, a *dhikr* (recitation) on the Prophet Muhammad, *salla 'ilahu 'alayhi wa sallam*, to do throughout, a determination to keep working with poetry and later drawing and its coloring, taking as my models those Zen masters who have presence of mind to deliver deathbed poems, and my beloved William Blake, who sang of his visions up to his death, executing gorgeously watercolored drawings of Dante's *Divine Comedy* in the final bed of his life. But I didn't go anywhere near that point in fact, and only felt true misery the weeks following the final chemo therapy and radiation session, when the body is left vibrating with the sum of all those treatments, working out its happiest response but convinced it will never really feel well again. I wrote poems, illustrated and published *The Crown of Creation*, and when I couldn't really write any poems for some reason, drew what I took to be healing pictures, in pen and ink and later colored with pencils. This book, with selected drawings published in black & white except for the cover, is the result of that work.

The drawings came after the illustrations, when I'd hit upon a kind of abstract vocabulary of shapes and jigsaws, extending in front of and behind one another, the first shapes drawn spontaneously, and unthinkingly, then wrapped and wreathed around with a certain tension and clarity between them, whose intense focus really lifted me from my physical state, and cornered me into solutions in linear composition and color that had a healing effect on me. Others might make harmoniously symmetrical Jungean mandalas, or even more elegant, Arabic calligraphies from Qur'an (and I should be embarrassed that I did not), but somehow these were the natural ways of my palliation, along with nothing more than a regular regime of acetametaphine that actually reduced tongue and throat ache.

It became alchemy. The chemicals that scoured through me, scrubbing and destroying, targeting the culprits but with collateral damage, didn't come directly from an alchemist's laboratory, but God is the major alchemist, His creations at all times under His command, our hurts and our healings, our diseases and cures, and His methods might be gentle or harrowing, and the results final for some, but this time, for me, I was reprieved, if not redeemed, and alchemically I must say, in my interior knowledge, more golden. Much gunk was begone'd. And while I may not yet be totally radiant, I have had light shed on me, *alhamdulillah*, for which I can only be grateful.

I'm overjoyed with the world, because the world is overjoyed from Him.
I'm in love with the whole universe because the whole universe is from Him.

Make the most of this Jesus-like breath of the dawn
that gives life to the dead heart, since this moment's breath is from Him.

Neither does the heavenly sphere possess it, nor do the angels.
That which is in the hidden core of the human heart is from Him.

I will gladly drink poison since the witness is the Winegiver.
I will devotedly endure the pain since the cure is from Him.

If the bloody blows do not let up, they will get better.
Delightful are such blows for which, at each instant, my salve comes from Him.

For one who knows God, how can there be any difference between sadness and happiness?
O Winegiver, pour some brew, happiness is that this sadness is from Him.

King and beggar are the same to us,
Since beneath this gate everyone's worshipping back is bent by Him.

Sa'di, though the flood of *fana* may sweep away the heart's house,
Keep your heart strong, since the foundation of *baqa* is made firm by Him.

— Sa'di *(translated by Shaykh Abdalhaqq Godlas)*

---

fana: annihilation in God
baqa: subsistence in God

GOD OF THE SPLINTER

O God of the splinter that fells a giant
of the gnat that burrows into the

brain of Nimrod
(such a famous drilling to Glory)

Of a spiraling tornado that flattens towns
but is the DNA's motion one

spinning spiral inside another

Of a bridge across water so dark
only the blind can cross it with

little consternation

God of antelope and antlers
squid and their inky shields

elephants and their lumbering bulk
humankind with every

weapon in the book
bent on self-destruction

Yet You've given into our hearts
the architectural structure of purest

incandescence to establish love zones of
total beneficence

on the sides of hills
in the midst of bomb blast

on this planet in its collision course with
endlessness and the Light You light

O God Who's put us in the
deep end to start with

and we must climb to the shallows
to stand knee deep with

saints in their beatitudes as the
churning waters of peacefulness

prevail

5/10

ANGELIC SHOES

The shoemaker saw that
angelic shoes miraculously

surrounded his feet
a perfect fit

The hoop flyer soared up and through
with the greatest of ease

the whole sky

opening its curtains so she could
land on her feet on the

other side in a
sea of clouds

The flautist floated his
breath through his flute and out the

open end
a whole symphony flowed

backed by a thousand-person choir in
blue tuxedos and flouncy blue gowns

There's really no end to the
miracles once just a little one comes into focus

Once we see everything fluttering its
miraculous wings

elephants finally look down at us from their
domed heights with

benign approval having always
seen things this way from the

start

Dust rises as they move off and as its
dirt flakes fall back to earth they

spell out jungle scriptures of such
monumental delicacy whole

populations close their books and
act on their advice of

elegantly symmetrical crystals and
the generous boon given us of

atomic structures by God the Most
Generous Giver

until even the most inert ones on earth
are seen to be dancing

5/11

GOOD CHEER AMONG THE CYNICS

Good Cheer came and
sat among the cynics

"What evidence do you have?" they asked
putting on snarl cougar masks and

long piggy moose faces

"None that you can see" sang Good Cheer
"though it land on you like a piano"

They sat still as a piano landed on them
proof of their position

even though it was playing a
gorgeous new sonata

*"That darkness we see
lays on us like gabardine"* they chanted

gleefully

*"The darkness you see is only
a play of light"* sang back Glee

There's no end to this drama and the
back and forth between them

and the cynics have convincing
evidence on their side it's true

but when the dust clears
do you see ruins or new shapes

and can anything God brings be
imperfect?

Even though the angels who bring things
look like they've been stung by wasps and

beaten up by psychopaths?

Conceive of a world
through this one

better than this one

Live in it

Stretch out your hand

and decorate it with
fairy lights

for all our own and
your own

well-being

SHORT FABLE OF THE THREE SCHOONERS

The first sailboat out had
nowhere to go but forward

out into pure *outness*

The light slitted down in louvered
doors that swung open for it to

enter
and enter it did

The second sailboat out saw things
differently and tacked to the

side and so slid along the
light in such a way it

slid out of sight

The third sailboat out lost
sight of the fact of the outing

and its sails fell slack
winds blowing elsewhere to fill

sails that would
respond to the air attack

The first boat and its green crew
sailed on into God's domain

His own breath pulsing them
onward and onward

in divine Flame

There's no record of the
other two schooners

They are probably goners

May God grant them honors

5/13

SEEING THE SCAFFOLD

Seeing the scaffold at the end of the road
or a steamroller coming toward you

or a herd of elephants bearing down
or looking into the maw of a tiger

on your morning stroll

his teeth and back of throat
and his greater existence

about to surround you
and all around you palm trees

sway and water still
rushes to its destination and

birds fly into branches and
continue to sing in fact

the whole universe is now a
polyphonic birdsong some trilling

happily some crooning mournfully
light playing its kaleidoscope patterns

around you accelerating and
brightening in gorgeous flashes

and the music of the spheres has finally
broken through the clouds

into your ears
as your

heart's about to break
and death take you

and the procession of saints can be
glimpsed over the hill

for you to join at the end
to continue on

past this world's din

5/15

ALL MOVING FORWARD IN TIME

It's all moving forward in time
All horses' noses create the finish line

Each flame tip tickles the
underbelly of heaven

Each heart of ours is the plate glass
to eternity's inner rooms

When we stand the whole universe
increases its stature

circulating its moons

It's all moving forward in time
All horses' noses create the finish line

If our blood didn't pound the
oceans would grow still

All roads begin when we
put our feet on the ground

A moment has passed but we
don't see it moving

What you hear in the air are its
waves in the inner ear

crashing infinity's shores

It's all moving forward in time
All horses' noses create the finish line

Inside us the Tree of Life
blooms and dies

Inside the Tree of Life
loftier skies blaze

See them now or lose the
taste of them forever

Our innermost branches
sweep their mirror

for their light
to pour down

It's all moving forward in time
All horses' noses create the finish line

At the base of my tongue a
foreign population produces sons

looking for territory to expand
a wild agenda

God's blessings on all of us
felt along the knobs of

our spines

In the strange land of ourselves
the victory's already won

It's all moving forward in time
All horses' noses create the finish line

I'm running out of time
You go on ahead to the finish line

All horses' noses create the finish line

5/17

SWEAT AND BOILS

We're all sweat and boils
sweat and scabs

scraping with potsherds

The whole thing comes down
while irony and nonchalance

abound around us

The isolation spotlight
hits us hard

Rimbaud said *"Patience is the key
to this savage sideshow"*

God takes away everything
but Himself

And now standing face to Face
what do we say

Some say Job said *"Enough!"* But
it's never enough

until it's all gone

Our nothingness is the dust

that rises around us

―――――――――――

I'm afraid to stand up
dizziness might knock me down

There's no way
to say this

I must refuse my self
and look for Mercy

5/18

VENETIAN MAGICIANS

Venetian magicians in their
satin pantaloons conjuring

flames out of ferns and fountains out of
pots

against a backdrop of Vesuvius

Rolling roils of ocean boiling
over us in rare rags of surf bubbles

until we swirl with dolphins and
speak their squeaks and trills

The earth itself opening up and
swallowing us whole

Ah this life with its flags always at
half mast and wild winds

blowing them to tatters

and the cups in our hands with their
soothing liquids and the

windows we look out of and the
windows we look in

Is it between our in and out breaths that
Paradise inflates and all

darkness expires?

At the moment of
each eyeblink when

our lids are closed that
a near vision of the Next World's

garden drapes its vines and
opens its opulent avenues?

The Venetian magicians take a bow
and the curtains close

The roiling ocean pokes its waves in the
air and flattens them at our

feet as we walk earth's lateral beaches
looking for gold

God's given us a door that we
only need open when the

need arises which is
always

And the road abruptly ends
which is now

5/19

PRAYER

Oh Allah

Let me have no fear
but only love for You

with every blow

                                                                       5/19

LAST AND FIRST WORDS

The last pen writes the last word
just as the first pen wrote the

first word and

both in the same penman's hand
on the same

pinnacle in space turning
silence into gold and

gold into sight and sound
for all to read and

hear

Goats on a hill even
turn to listen and

clouds gather overhead as
people stream into and

out of the domain of first and
last words

all from the same wordsmith
on the one pinnacle

singing the heart's song and

sounding its once-silent gong

with wave bands extending their
circles in space to unite both

first and last words in their
sonic rounds

And we're born and die in
first and last words

with all the jump-ropes in between
grammatically arranged in their

perfect and imperfect strands
the way DNA sings in our

cells from first to last
and past our

own existence
stretching out

throughout
time

5/23

MY MOTHER

My mother
who is both bruised and whole

vulnerable and strong
waits for me on a cloud

She will put on Grand Opera dress
and bellow out a song

or whimper a whisper
along unused telephone wires

to be heard above the crowd

She doesn't ride a dragon's back
nor stand gigantic among a

million suns blazing in a
black sky

She was deft and dwarf-like
not really dwarf-like but

delicate and like a bruised
magnolia petal or something

turned slightly brown at the edges

I can see her physical shape in my
mind's eye

spiritualized

She's patient and self-absorbed
loving in her usual way

both strong and a bit
dithering

although her late Alzheimer's is
gone and she

knows her surroundings and
where she should be

and is right there
where she should be

waiting for me
and has seen for herself now

what it's all about

No one's agnostic in heaven
the Next World can be a

brutal awakening
and the

radiance there
blinding by tearing the

blinders off completely

Maybe she rides a white horse
among a herd of

similar riders
among the clouds

She could be
beckoning me

but she isn't
now that she

knows for herself

She waits
all by herself

patiently

for me

5/25

IF I SHOULD DIE TONIGHT

If I should die tonight
it would be like stepping out onto a big pond's

lily pads with all the other frogs

combing out my hair and its
flames falling onto a plate

the horse muzzle that follows me
finally coming so close I can

feel its breath
sweet as clover all over me and the

sheer delight of simply galloping

Hills become flat and
broad valleys rolling

Sky melts back into its
first kaleidoscope

rotating its rainbows

White gloves handle me
and swans crowd the air with an

avalanche of feathers rising on its

updrafts

I'd say goodbye to everything at once
and hello to God Who would

come through the aether to catch me
afloat as always but now with even

greater buoyancy

Let giraffes crowd around my bed
their sexy eyelashy eyes shining as the

whole bed rises

and all the windows of the world
open of their own accord

to let me out into the sound of
tubular bells and gurgling waters and

newborns opening their eyelids for the
first time and

looking around
their inner light blending with the

light they've been born into
where everything happens and

nothing happens

in the instant of our lives and deaths

but this
sudden awakening

5/25

POEM BEGUN WITH A LINE BY THOMAS TRANSTRöMER

> *Death is the mother of beauty*
> — Wallace Stevens, *Sunday Morning*

At the smuggling of the dead across
the border

and the gypsy boatman in his
transparent tatters

himself transparent

and everyone in line one by one
waiting to cross

and the faces in their solemnity
telling their secret tales

powdered into sheer beauty by the
blue winds of Mercy

everyone holding onto their tickets
written in Sanskrit

listening in their ears to the
first language of Adam

peacocks screeching through the vowels
whales butting their

heads against the consonants

the mirror of the sky bending down
to reflect our souls back to us

as we wait to cross
now the mist encircling us

one by one

and the elemental bond in
all our hearts beginning to

beat out the rhythm of light that
binds us

5/28

THE LIONS' ARENA

The lions' arena
is full of medical equipment

The roar of the lions is the
great radiation ring whirring

The crowd leaning forward with
thumbs at the ready

wears chemotherapy gowns

It's a hot day
and a restless hum is in the air

The masks of everyone's faces
are beginning to slip

As we enter naked and
shackled the

crowd is hushed

The outcome is anyone's guess
and God's to toss into the

arena's dust we've
been since birth

waiting for this moment's
test

There's no signal to start
all is already closing in

A star glimmers overhead
for each of us

wanting the best

Our hearts have already
entered paradise

and come to
rest

5/28

SCIENCE FACT SCIENCE FICTION

If illness by Allah is science fact

then its cure is
science fiction by a mad

scientist we hope's on the right track

his beakers abubble his machinery abuzz

the light in the air growing youthful
peach fuzz

a pasture of health in the distance
waiting for us

to arrive in one piece and
run on its grass

into the open space
of His Merciful Face

5/28

I HEAR NEARBY

> *Allah dressed them with His own clothes*
> *and He took them in His high protection*
> — Ibn al-Husayn al-Sulami
> (Kitab al-Futuwwah)

I hear nearby
firing squad bullets

meant for me

I am elsewhere

All my deeds in a little box
in my heart

There are trees in full leaf
and meadows in full bloom

Nothing ripples like a horse's back
bounding through the air

I soar over oceans
to get nearer to sky

the waves below
don't even see me go

Though the bullets get nearer
I'm their superior

My metal harder than theirs
my swift spirit swifter in dispersal

I'm already air

Only God is near
nearer and nearer

They whistle as they work
coming toward me

But my whistle is higher
and clearer

Whole cities have risen and
fallen into ruin

and not a moment has passed
whole populations disappeared

and appeared again
all different faces

and all the same spirit

Nothing really disappears
once it is

I think they're about to
reach their mark

but I'm not there

I'm wearing
God's underwear

5/29
(morning of first Chemo & radiation therapies)

POEM ENDING WITH LINES BY YEATS

I've got a dark force swimming inside me
sort of like the Beast from the Black Lagoon

or the famous statue of Lacoön with
everyone's limbs entangled in snakes

and its phosphor eyes and sulfur breath
are searching out the little blobs that are

trying to kill me

as it swims through all my
pipes and passages ransacking

(sadly) even some of the good Samaritans inside who just
happen to be nearby where the cowardly

dastards are dividing with no
rhyme or reason

and the dark force this time is my
new lover injected by angels in

scientific smocks and its gnashing
teeth are looking for detritus to bite

(I've always wanted to use that
word in a poem I pronounced

debt-tritus after my California mother's pronunciation
but in a poem New Jersey's Allen Ginsberg once read

he pronounced it de-*try*-tus so it's
up for grabs)

slithering through every crack and opening
putting its tiny massive head where

no light shines to find the floating
crap game of cancerous cells where they

attach themselves this time at the
base of my only tongue

and smash them to smithereens
foreclosed and forgotten

dispelled in the drainage system of my
only body back into the

black sea from which they came
the both of them finally reduced to a

tiny point of light above a sloshing
brackish harbor

water lapping with low sounds by the shore
in the deep heart's core

5/29

ALL'S WELL

All's well
in Cancer Ward Dell
as far as I can tell

Drip drip goes the
drip machine
Life is but a dream

It's four in the morn
I'm a bit forlorn
Gabriel blow your horn?

5/30

In Islam the angel Israfil blows the horn of Resurrection.
I'm echoing the Cole Porter song and the western view.

ALLAH

Allah Allah Allah
What are You doing

but what You do

And who are we to complain?

5/30

THE CHEMO

The chemo
is sinking into the loam of me

5/30

I ENTER A HUGE TEMPLE

I enter a huge temple

It's built in the shape of the
hidden Name of God

mostly glass
four visible rivers through the walls

surround it

The stewards of the temple are a
mile tall

They look down at me in rows
as I enter

Their glances wash me

From somewhere comes the odor of
cooking meat

intermingled with incense
and the intoning of song

Song unlike ever heard before
in intermingling waves

The walls resound and echo it all

changing landscapes

shifting waters
whisperings around

my own form as I enter
one step at a time in decelerating

motions
everything assuming a kind of

physical hush
except the crackle in the air

from a distant source

and everywhere the sense that
there's no one in charge here

but Allah

no one in
charge but Light

my own body
made of glass

with nothing inside it
but Light

and the faint odor of incense

intermingled with the floating odor of

cooking meat
intermingling with the

highest sweetness

5/31
(3 a.m. 2nd night after first chemo and one anti-nausea Zofran)

JOB SITS IN HIS CHAIR

Job sits in his chair of molten lead
walks on a beach of burning sand

speaks words that blister the air
sings a soft song that his

heart can hear

Finds his closest companion just
a jugular vein away

Holds onto that conversation as its
whirlwind hurls its lights

through the entire rattletrap cosmos
returning again as earth-shattering music

whose gong is himself
going over Niagara in the

barrel of his ribcage
holding on as it crashes through the

waves in spattering sprays of
silver and gold sparks

against a flashing blue sky that flies from
Hell to Paradise in a single arc

on which Job rides as if on a stallion
loosed from its pen its tail aflame

with everything in the world he's
known and loved

whipping the air itself into
screens of fire

onto which his whole life plays
from moment to moment from his first birth

to the time he now finds himself in
aswelter in pure being

facing God's Face like breath
blown on a windowpane

clearing to a transparency
where Job and windowpane both

vanish completely away
and God alone stays

6/2

FALLING

If a body starts to fall
and there's nothing to stop it falling

how long will it fall
and through how many worlds?

The visions of our hearts pass in a
whooshing whirl

The sounds in our ears of every
symphony ever heard every

conversation exchanged every
trilling bird

The wind rushes past us
coming from in front

And if we start falling apart
but the soul is whole

how will it go?

Will the soul come forth with
bravado?

Or a wisp of intense light that
contains us whole?

The worlds of the past are gone
except for their gongs

going on

And this one crowds around us

And the next one's unknown
except what the Prophet's shown

Our souls chime in fear and delight to
know firsthand when

this life is gone

and the body has no more
to fall

and God is all

6/2

A LITTLE BLUE MONK

A little blue monk in a purple
cassock served us sarsaparilla

He looked through eyes that had been
through a thousand years of blinking

I think to him we resembled chrysanthemums
in colored vases

He wept as he told us his joys
and how the light irradiated his little

cell at night and how soft the
voices and deep the import

A faqir came along in a yellow *djellaba*
and brought tame giraffes to ride

*"These are swifter than most and one
bound takes us to the far horizon*

*to the rising or setting sun — whichever
you wish"*

We rode all day and the sun rose
successively for love was in the

air and nothing could stop us from

diving right into it and through its
heartfelt syrups

A little Buddha appeared and held his
hand above his head to indicate we'd

arrived at the right location

for his feet knew each terrain as perfect
and he knew for us what was

perfect for our feet as well
as we looked out over the sheerest

canyons for miles and miles we'd
ever seen

and from the depths of their crevasses rose
colored streamers and

rays of golden light

and the voices here assured us we'd
arrived at the appropriate place

When we looked around there was
no one there but we were

not alone

and a Face of Light floated in the

air in front of us
to show us our souls

6/3

THE ROWERS

The rowers of the big boats
had no letup

The trapeze artist has to
catch his mate

for once in midair it's
too late to be

elsewhere

A mortal born must go on
until there's no more

going on

then continues by his
Fashioner in His fashion

to where his Fashioner has
fashioned

Those explorers who went to the
ends of the earth and

perished in their tents

their own bodies their last frail

physical refuge

as the sleet continued to fall
the final resounding chord on the

planet's piano played

Alone in our beds
the brush against the

cheek of that nearness
having been born into

physical being it's
too late to be elsewhere

Having nothing at all to do with the
body is the saint's way

of astounding conviction
and God's direct Light

falling upon them
head to toe

inside and out

Looking over the edge of things
can we see any other way out?

But row the big boat

catch wrists in

midair
be peaceful in our

icy tents

bodiless Allah
our sole refuge?

6/4

THE SOUL

The soul is a
flowering peach tree blooming on a

bright green hill

The scale of a dragon fallen into the
Princess' goblet turning water into the most

effluvious Paradisiacal wine one sniff of which up our
nostrils turns our flesh to song

A harbor full of sailing vessels each
loaded with inestimable treasure

but in the eyes of a single child
nothing but a cloth doll or a

lump of clay
treasured more than all the rest

and the evaluation is true

We crash against our souls with the most
unmannerly manners

yet its High C transcends all the
cacophony we produce

It's calmer than smooth ocean under
moonlight in a sweet island cove

has traveled farther than the most
outlandish shaman from the

wildest frontier with his hard-won
healing song bringing the

entire village back to life and seals
back swimming under the ice

Is cooler than breezes over Ganges
burning ghats that take Hindus'

bodies' essences in fine ash flakes to the
godliest heavens to

dance with other souls forever
in their extravagant eternity

Is hotter than gypsies' *cante hondo* on makeshift
wood tables in heart-echoing forests of their only

safe refuge

We can never sing enough to our souls
to encourage their bravado while our

bodies seem to simmer in their
own juices or

disintegrate all around us bit by bit
like forest animals one by one running back

into the coziness of their lairs

leaving us like lone singers on a
single hill at midnight under

an entire sky of silver stars

Our souls in the pockets of our
deepest beings waiting to be

lured into the open to
prove themselves victorious over

all
and over all and anything

that can hit us
however it may hit us

to leave us truly and undauntedly
victorious

after all

6/5

SMALL TOWN

The spines of the small town
chime against the night

and the fires of the small town
crackle in their hearths

and the people of the small town
thrive and wax and wane

according to their strengths

and the gremlin of the small town
coughs behind his grate

and the angel of the small town
looks between its clouds and blows

blessings to their hearts
from its vast dimensionless place

and the people turn their faces to where
someone usually is

to ask the way to where
no one is a stranger

in the labyrinthine streets
lit by flickering lamps

and the beast outside the doors
bellows silently

its huge face turned to
everyone's birth star

out in space

and all of this presided over by
God's Compassionate Eye

Who holds the perfect globe of it
in everyone's perfect heart

aloft among the prostrations of
His most obedient angels

held suspended in a
single drop of light

6/6

THE FIRST TWO LINES CAME DURING RADIATION # 7

A field of corn brings us
the deliciousness of sunlight

A gushing stream brings us the
curvature of our blood

Multitudes of people traveling their
tortured roads bring us the

meandering of our thoughts

whose focus on a setting sun brings us
the beauty of finality to

this life and our lives and all
living creatures until

God brings the sun up to His
All-seeing Eyes again and we

continue as before for as
long as He deems worthy

breathing His air on His earth
in all the

footsteps He's ordained
for us

HOW MANY SIRENS MORE

How many sirens more will I hear
before I die

or the dew hitting the upsides of
leaves and quivering grass blades at dawn

which I don't really hear but can
well imagine makes tiny pings when it

does and it
definitely does

as space itself lightens from dense
star-packed black to something

infinitely lighter and generally sunny
drying that first dew undone

while out on some street sirens
wail wild grieving laments

and they could be counted from this very
moment I heard one pass to when I

myself will pass with
how many overheard

wailing sirens
in between?

SOUL QUESTIONS

Do the soul's arms hang
down at its sides?

Do the soul's legs
extend down from its hips?

Do the soul's eyes
float above sea level?

Do they see to the ends of
creation and scan the great

globe of its ethereal atmospheres?

Does the soul's nourishment
enter the mouth and circulate

among its delicious caverns?

Are the soul's lengths and
breadths and widths the

whole sky's peak and oceans'
mysteries?

Are the creatures of the soul as
familiar with us as

we are with ourselves?

Do the cries of the soul
reverberate inside God's Throne

and come back merciful music?

Does the rain of the soul
wet grasses and delicate

tips of cypress trees?

Is the soul in the shadow of a
doorway and

sunlight along a fence?

Eyes of the soul meet
eyes of the One Soul

and do they fill with
tears of recognition and

uttermost familiarity?

Does the soul go
out across expanse

and continue in endlessness?

Does the soul's heart beat with the
same heartbeat our

bodies have harbored since before we were
born?

Is the soul's heartbeat now
God's heartbeat

that is no heartbeat we can know?

Will we see the wasteland below us
and the Glad Land before us?

Is air the skin of the soul
and Light its soul

recalling it back to itself
to send out its pulse

where we have never
gone before?

Eyes open wide
the soul's deep inner abode

its ever-alive
abiding?

6/9

WHAT FIRE PREVENTED

1

The circus let out early and the
elephant sat in her cage

Clowns removed their white to their natural
pink or brown underneath

The contortionist stretched out for a
lengthy nap

along his entire length
as normal as anyone supine

Josie the tightrope walker walked between the
caravans puffing on her forbidden

cigarette in the slight haze of this
tropical afternoon

The giraffes' heads towered above the
caravan roofs and the

village children from afar delighted in their
phantasmal shapes

All is well on the circus grounds
and nothing is afoot

No skullduggery or malfeasance no
shady dealings or larcenous absconding

but only a usual afternoon among these
unusual folk for whom a

nice afternoon off though somewhat
rare is a welcome and

calming respite to an otherwise
irregular and certainly offbeat if not

downright
bohemian life

2

When the fire broke out
the lion was asleep

What no one knew was that an
entire angelic order had been

assigned to watch over the circus
because of the child born to the Argentinean

trapeze artists who at
the time were picnicking with their

five children at the

edge of the grounds

the saintly baby in a
basket surrounded by birds

*A loud crack as the main
tent pole splits in two!*

*A great roaring bellow as the canvas
in the main tent catches fire!*

Smoke billows above the
circus as if phantom hippopotamus

herds are riding down the sky
though on each billow an

angel rides to keep the
flames from harming a single soul

as everyone awakes or runs in their
panic to the water buckets

always at the ready for such
emergencies

Cries and shouts of the
circus performers and crew

pulling animal wagons away
calling to each other through

chugging billows of
brown smoke

3

The flames resembled leaping lions
jabbing snakes

relentless in their attacks and hot
counterattacks

a vicious darkness where there'd
been ebullient light and

tuba *oompahs* and flight through hoops

But while Hell seems to have
opened up at this happy circus

what's fascinating is the
angelic squadrons fanning

out in the unseen to save each soul
suddenly making real

feats of daring and aerial acrobatics
that by the circus performers seemed now

comparatively so
earthbound

Billions of angels came in phalanges and filed in
troops between the fire and all the

people and beasts

They tumbled through belches of smoke
and flew in the rafters' heights as well as

at the low level of wagon wheels and
floppy clowns

combating sheets of fire with their
angelic ice

lessening its outraged effects
against the innocent joys of

brightly painted matter
suddenly vulnerable to the

disease of burning

for that one precious baby destined to
shine in the eternal worlds as

saint and messenger among us

same as that spot of perfection in our
bodies unscorched by any

outbreak and surrounded by

angelic air invulnerable to its

flames

That sea of light in the
clenched ball of darkness that is

our mortal being
doomed to incinerate in its

brightness

that flying baby in the
wild circus of our being

angelically protected
that leads us into God's

cool asbestos atmospheres beyond all
conflagration

the leaping sweet roar of it made more
agile than even death's

deep earthly plodding

4

Josie sat on a coil of
uncharred rope and unburnt pulleys

and noticed how frayed the
rope was in places and how

close it had been to breaking

The clowns went through the
remains of their

dressing room tents and noticed for the
first time the old tins of clown white's

ingredients
included poisonous lead

The saved heap of nets the flames missed
showed signs of rot

The trapeze artists with the saintly
child saw their old but unscorched rigging

had been about to shred
as they coughed their way to where it

lay in ropey zigzags across the dirt

But the old main tent was flakes of
ashen canvas

The wooden center rings were black dust

The lion lay asleep on his huge paws

The elephant gazed through slow wise
eyes at her fifth disaster since

Madras

as the circus performers saw the
fire saved them from worse calamities

thank God

and another day dawned and the
circus put itself back together as

best it could
and moved on

6/10-11

CANCER

Cancer creeps in on little cat's feet

Cancer grows from the root upward

Cancer as a fact is a hard fact to grasp

Cancer wears no mask but hides in
private places

Cancer greedily drinks at the oasis meant for
healthy beasts and weary travelers

Cancer's dark generosity knows no bounds

Cancer is that thing that once planted
can't easily be got rid of except through
foreclosure or death

Cancer rides death's black horse
but should be walking beside it

When cancer appears everything changes
as if death were drawing nearer
when it's God drawing nearer

Cancer is a sown field full of
tares and rocks trying to
flourish at the farmer's expense

Somehow there's no sky above cancer
but only the closeness of a closed room
and a small expandable exit

that could become sky

Cancer thinks its attitude is
our attitude but it
won't get away with it

Cancer is a man in a blue blazer
waiting at the corner for a
man in a black trench coat but
when they meet the man in blue will
blaze and open up into a
night full of stars

Cancer clings like a monkey
sings like a drunken sailor
rings like a giant bronze bell
in the Pure Land of the Buddha

Cancer is the clearest indicator of
Who is in charge
that He might wipe it away
little by little

until we are clean again

or as never before

ACCEPTABLE

The call from across the water
to come to the edge and

peer over the edge

to see what no one else but you can
see

there among the clonging xylophones of
clouds and shift-changing mists that

form matter and then dissolve it
change after change

Huge hulls of boats looming
sightings of unbefore-known continents

lying like great tortoise backs under
baking suns in the

slosh of endless surf

But we peer farther and faster
burning in our own fires

not the castle of ice there
nor the world of a whirling tornado

that picks everything up and
displaces it

but peer farther and faster
past all this

past the nostrums of disaster
pulled by the call of it

out of our own self's plaster

to the liquefaction of desire
the melt that spells the

antidote to fire
in which we dwell whole and

unsacrificed on mortality's pyre

upright in Light's satisfied embrace

— *acceptable*

6/13

WISDOM

Wisdom comes in hard chunks
or slow rivers

floods a city and
pushes houses into the sea

breaks through roofs in the
form of a saintly person

drifting slowly
among us

crashes cars into a mountain
and the mountain

tunnels into Light

Over and over our hands
waver above a chessboard

Then one day without warning
the right move is made

Our reflection in the mirror
speaks more eloquently than we do

Allah's Voice
louder than our own

Streets are paved with gold
when our eyes see them so

The language of birds is comprehensible
when our ears are attuned

Our hearts fly in wisdom's atmospheres
up front with the pilot

looking out over the stars

Any dark alley may
turn into a thoroughfare

poplars on each side and a
brass band down the middle

If wisdom is *"the lost riding beast
of the believer"*

we must search in the
mists on our own two feet

until we ride it again

and God's peace on us
opens our galloping eyes

6/13

ONE VOICE CALLING US

There's no more room for me Lord
there's only room for You

A mountain peak against the sky
sky in a glass of water

Ocean in a single drop
Dawn pours out of a rooster

The road unrolls as we roll along
A landscape fills a window

Everywhere we look there's only light
we've disappeared in the aether

I hear a wheel turning
and it's the world

I hear the world turning
and it's a wheel

There's a voice inside an echo
calling us one by one

One voice calling us
and we're alone

6/17

THE BODY

1

Two bandy legs
sticking out below

from crotch to top of head —
my body

No koala in these limbs
no sloths upside down

all organs inside squished
perfectly as meant

created to mobilize and speak
walk and lie down

breathe air and die

2

My body
sweet soul-encasing pod

your wheels of feet having
transported me to here

hospital where fluids
down transparent plastic

tubing to the
tune of a machine's soft ticking

drip by drip
chemo accompaniment

seething and searching out
those multi-multiplying

cells

Hell's bells

3

My body from the start

rubbery baby flesh now
elongated and wrinkly in

the oddest places
arm skin like parchment

but I remember the
tart taste I'd suck till gooey

of the leather strap my mother

buttoned under my

chin to clasp my
ear-flapped hat on

and how it felt so snug
on this same head

4

Body who's taken me
Egypt Morocco Nigeria

Mecca Medina
near saintly precincts

as well as flesh's
sensory delights that

got me into this pickle
chemotherapy the cure

an old cured pickle this
body for sure

5

In extremes of distress
we can't just

up and leave our body
like exiting a gas station's

stinky bathroom
shutting the door

behind us

into world's air
fresh and clear

Smeared bleared
the body's

bread and blood
however

deftly it conspires
against us

ours the tent in which
life's gaudy circus

plays in life's
gaudy circus

6

Outside the body
inside the body

God's Unity is met

I wanted to say
silver and blue

a blue so intense it's
not blue

a silver so silver it
shivers

6/19
Lankenau Hospital (during 24 hr. chemo treatment)

LEANING MY HEAD ON MY HAND

I'm leaning my head on my hand
trying to think super realistically

about my situation

Chemo-hiccups have stopped
(brought on by anti-nausea medication)

I've just prayed *fajr* and asked for
healing for a long list of people

near and far and for
myself from the Single Healer of us

all and I'm about to
get more sleep *insha'Allah*

hoping I'll be able to eat some
breakfast (throat getting rough and

raw — *mucositis*) and food
unappetizing (low-grade nausea)

There's a heat wave outside my
open screen door

going up to 100°

It's Friday and my
radiation session is my

Jum'ua

through heat wave to an
intensely focused blast of radiant

x-rays (I'm off on weekends)

no hair loss and weight loss seems
minimal so far

Misery laps at the shore
but I won't let it

slurp towards me

Time to pick up my
rattles and sing to my

tongue cancer an improvised
shaman song of loving eradication

Prayer on the Prophet
patting the place on my throat

Light inside and out
stronger than it is

God doesn't lie

I'm done with The Lie

He's *al-Hayyu al-Qayyum*
and I'm *Abd* al-Hayy

                                                               6/22

---

fajr - Dawn Prayer
insha'Allah - If God Wills
Jum'ua - Friday Congregational Prayer
al-Hayyu al-Qayyum - God's Names: The Living, The Sustaining
Abd - slave or servant (of The Living)

DARK CHEMO THOUGHTS

What is a dead thing?
A thing that does not move

and like burnt wood
charred and black?

How are we thus
elongated in eternity?

Eyes sealed heart stopped
mouth that spoke and

ears that heard
hands at our sides now

legs full out and still

all silent

Yet I conceive of it here
on the life side

looking at my live hand
writing it out

yet seeing myself thus

Not morbid thoughts

but how many are we?

Alive now in earthly form
but not forever

There's no end
and death is not an end

though we see plants die that
don't return

and dead birds on the road
no more in flight

rocks and stones

Where are the voices coming from
that lift us

out of this abyss?

In chemo-misery these
thoughts obtrude

and the Garden
tenuous

6/22

A RAGE OF BRAVERY

I flew into a rage of bravery
before being hit by a

raging storm of dull ache and
mouth wrack

insisting no misery would fell me
this tree God's granted me to be

whose core I swore and
still swear

is Light
though sight of it

less bright

in the reality of physical
disrepair

I see hope's green leaves
where no green shows

and pity the hopeless
in their colorless throes

of despair

6/23

ONLY ONE THING

All the bad we've done
all the good

comes to only one thing
love of God

    6/23

NEWSPAPER FANTASY

I opened the newspaper this
morning and all the

type slid off onto my lap

I rearranged it to read:
Angels Sighted Over Major Cities

*When radios were turned on this
morning all that was heard*

was celestial music

*Penguins have sent their
first representatives to the UN*

*Whale speech decoded and their
good counsel received*

*Firearms all over the world have
melted now combat is only*

hand to hand

*Nuclear Powers can't find their
warheads for their*

warheads have vanished

Today no one raised their voice
and good words were heard by all

A bit puerile perhaps but far
better than the usual news

6/25

WRITTEN IN PARKING LOT AFTER RADIATION SESSION

I saw an old man all skin and bones
who made no cry and moaned no moans

Stretched out full length upon the street
barely clothed no shoes on feet

The Buddha saw such a man as he
but this time around that man was me

6/25

HIS MOST PRECIOUS CONCERN

> (*salla 'llahu 'alayhi wa sallam* is assumed after the mention of his blessed name)

The Prophet Muhammad sits by the
bedside of the sick

Stands in our doorways to
shield us from the light

Strolls with us through our
dark woods

Is there in the clouds when we
fly in the air

and meets us when we
land at our differing destinations

Each one of us at once
his most precious concern

Messenger of God
not for a moment leaving us

comfortless

Feel his breath as he
bends over us

complete and deep assured

His full attention on the
condition of our souls

to pluck us from every
purgatorial indifference

*peace and blessings of
Allah be upon him*

greater than the sum
of each of our allotted breaths

and his Companions and Family
to the Next World

most true

6/28

EVER-OCEAN-FLOWING SPACE

The music that should unroll from
somewhere unrolls from

everywhere
whose Source is One

now playing multifarious
twanged notes through the dust bowl

to defibrillate the melancholy heart

or out of stretched leather over a
coffee can with strings on the

High Atlas in the snow with a
cracked but warbling voice sung by a

beggar in *djellaba* with high
opera intentions

to the sudden squall that just
floated by my window with its

spattering of xylophonic high and
low notes played on leaf-tops and

thunder stones

and every other music conceived or
inconceivable but produced out of

the universe's voice box with a
crash here and a

crescendo there until our own
dancing bodies are unfolded from their

silent centers through their tubular
corridors out every possible pore

into the constant glorious Godly
chimes of ever-opening and

ever-ocean-flowing
space

6/29

ALL OUR ATTEMPTS AT HEALING

"There's a cure for everything but death"
— Hadith of the Prophet *(salla 'llahu alayhi wa sallam)*

All our attempts at
healing are to elude the long

loving arms of death coming
around us

The doorway filling with a sulfurous
light or beneficent radiance

elongating its rays into our hearts
into this little living blip between

two eternities

and somehow from this perspective
all the hustle and bustle of

earth life and its being taken so
seriously becomes

symphonic but strange

We all rush to our appointments
but dread God's decreed most poignant one

on a Venetian canal under moonlight's

eerie glow and slosh of brackish water

or standing at ease in our usual
nonchalance with

nothing particular to do or think or
say

The mortal bubble we're
in and that's in us just such an

evanescence that we naturally
hold back from hearing pop

Our song should twirl around it
the most magnificent of roses

the simplest and most
heartfelt of songs

And may God give me the strength to
believe all this if the

corridor of my own cure becomes
too narrow to

fit down

and only the ocean of love alone
remains left

to wash me clean

IN THE DARK CASINO

Sort it all out God
I can't sort it out

I see a dark spy leaning on a
window ledge staring in

I see a road so shining
it hurts my eyes

I see my body with a
small but crucial territory

overtaken

Loving my loved ones is a
lifeline and their

loving back from their end
a heart-hold up the

unbannistered stairway

and the tropical birds on my
shoulders who speak in

perfect sentences

and the flickering outcome of all this
my allotted breaths

blinking their numbers on a
roulette wheel going too

fast to see
in the dark casino

7/1

THE BLOOM UPON THE ROSE

— in memoriam Sabura Nigro

The bloom upon the rose
saw itself and blushed

and the stem became thinner
than a hair

as The Gardener passed by
His tall shadow

crossing her mossy bed

and the sky above Him
where His name shines

among pale planets and stars
inched closer to bathe her

rosy face in His tears

from no farther away
than His breath upon her

petals one by one
in the noonday sun

7/2

OUR HURTS

Our hurts are lost in God's
starry skies among the more

angular constellations
roaring of lions and armed

warriors charging across emptiness

light years apart from their most
ferocious adversaries

like being lost at sea
surrounded by God's water

but humankind on a
far ship going elsewhere

Our hearts are so completely in
God's realm here

we can only sing songs to it
and take its pulse from

time to time in its
regular measures and

occasional eccentricities

But its care and handling
its corridors leading inward

its own tropical birdsong on Paradise branches
heard from time to time by our

less perfect ears

is God turning it as He pleases
inspecting its light among the

stellar luminaries
we so pray to be companion to

when the going gets rough
and the coming home to

God's starry skies
so sweetly desirable

7/3

ON THE SHEER SIDES OF THINGS

On the sheer sides of things
as well as the flats

in the deep abysses of things
as well as the peaks

in the clear perspective of things
as well as dissolving almost

completely away from clarity
into a mist so thick

rearrangement takes place
instantaneously

so Big Ben looms over Cairo
and the sphinx winks in

Picadilly Circus to passing motorcars

We're as fragile as those
light plastic feathery shuttlecocks

that get knocked over Badminton nets

more like Swiss cheese than a
rubbery capsule for

soul-wandering up
Forevermore's Trails

in all kinds of weather

It may desert us at anytime
though for the most part

treated with love and respect
indivisible from the soul itself

our bodies prove again and again
to be seaworthy crafts for crossing

the River Styx's
one-way trip

walk-worthy for traversing the blade-thin
Sirat pulled tight between

now and everywhere else

out of this world

7/5

Sirat: Bridge over the Fire of Hell in the Next World

VELVETS AND ICY METALS

The velvets that surround us
and the icy metals

in this perfect universe God's
placed us in

and the cool waters almost
everywhere or from

above or dug way down
and found at our feet

Jewels of earth crushed and
redolent

heat and cold proportional
caterpillar metamorphosis

everywhere in some bright
stage of transition

each breath curled like
fronds of ferns in our

spongy lungs
and the blood bath inside us

that keeps us continually

bathed

in the bath of life

And the life that eludes us
and the life we've got

crystals revolving to see through
in perpendicular perspectives

magic lantern flashes
on the inner person and the

outer where Allah's
Names have been stamped

indelibly in living color

from the uncoil to the
ultimate coil again

among unseen elements
that have always

nourished us
among velvets and

icy metals that
abound around us

and within us

YOUNG PICADILLY PEOPLE

> *Picadilly* from *piccadills* (17th cent., Spanish or Portuguese, also called *picadils* or *pickadils* — stiff collars with scalloped edges and a broad lace or perforated border)

Young Picadilly people
bordering on the insane

come back to the land of
silver lakes and small cascades

rock shelves of light ferns
the size of houses

refuge to your hearts
out of the fray

And you who hold the world so
close to your chests you can't

see it neither its
pitfalls nor its perpendicular

heights and coves of beauty
splendid sunsets and

flora beyond surprise

Neither this Age nor its
rat race need you to

grease its wheels with your
precious fluids

The Table of Grace needs you far
more lovingly to be among its

attendees in flesh and spirit

Don't look now
but the Great Shadow is

crossing near us
and the road does end

somewhere around here

7/7

THE FINITE SING OF THE INFINITE?

Can the finite sing of the infinite?
Can the miniscule sing of the magnificent?

A gnat know an eagle's fell swoop?

A stone in the road know a
canyon's majesty?

A drop view the
ocean's expanse even from its

round perspective?

A word encompass God's
encyclopedic language choir

spread everywhere on earth?

The light in these eyes
ever really know what another sees?

Our hearts like castles of light on
hills of light

gaze everywhere at once?

This world can't contain God's Light
but an alive heart can

Do we need to be granted
lions' eyes to see at night?

The road is gravel
all the way to the end

If we orient ourselves to Him
the rest comes flooding

If our perpendicular is to
God's domain we

needn't walk the earth
though our feet touch ground

Having been flung around the universe
to roll back down to a

central position again

If God's song is sung from our marrow bone
our skeleton becomes His xylophone

and our flesh His windblown sails
that will bring us home

TWENTY-EIGHT POEMS AGO

Twenty-eight poems ago I may have lost
track of a trapeze partner and not

caught her as she flew
toward me to be

caught by her wrists and I would
hope she might come through

literal space right now
to be so caught

Then there are numerous
savage beasts in my

poems that might be
out there somewhere roaming

around and
bothering the neighbors tigers of

fire and ice bears screeching peacocks
a number of astonished lions who don't

respond very well to being
intimidated by chairs

as well as essences emotions sentiments that

might be unresolvedly reverberating like

bronze bells with their
clappers removed and so though

seemingly silent to a passerby
actually clanging away in some

sidereal dimension or other

If possible to redeem these
and other loose ends I've

inadvertently activated I'd feel
grateful

though I suppose we all have
kick-started various energies that are

still traveling in Newtonian arcs in their
trajectories in space somewhere and we may be

forced to submit to the general
enervation of them simply

winding down of their
own accord and just

pray they behave as
best they can and pray that as

the hand-tied biological parents of our
actions may we face the

mortal doorway with as
few such loose ends as

possible and may our
partners be caught in midair and wild

animals pacified by the
singing Orpheus of our

intentions to organize as
much of our lives in

peaceable circles around us
on bright grassy mountainsides under

shaded cypress and larch trees
overlooking the world with

both silent and eloquent
calm

7/10

THE NIGHT IS A RED JACKET

The night is a red jacket
thrown over the back of a ghost

thrown over the back of a chair
in an overlit room of

overlit light

so neither ghost nor chair are
visible in the light

and vision continues
so far out among the stars

it comes back again
behind us

having circumnavigated the
exact shape of the universe

along its interior
outside side in

one swooping arc
worthy of supersonic

flight

that is actually
our heart in its

godly delight

7/10

FAITHFUL SLIPPERS

Faithful slippers here you are
waiting by the side of my bed

when I get up two hours after
falling asleep to pee

rundown strange two-tone black and
blue-gray leather Italian type slip-ons with

streamlined soft leather tops I got in
Turkey a few years back

and some thought were beautiful
and others the ugliest

shoes they'd ever seen
so I started wearing them as

indoor shoes in our shoeless
carpeted house

and here you are still
snug on my feet in this

Neruda-esque expostulation regarding your
humility of service all these

years and how I've been having to

glue the bottom sole onto the

top a number of times lately where it
flaps off and must be

fastened on again
and there is a metaphysic here somewhere I'm

sure about adherence and
down-to-earthness but they're

on my feet now and this
ode is nearly over and I

haven't gotten up yet from my
writing lap desk to do my

nightly office
slippered efficiently and may I say

lovingly by these two
having waited for two hours to be

so slipped into

7/12
(night after 3rd and final chemo)

WATER

Water in a jug of water
water in cascades of water

water in our body
keeps our body afloat

If we think of all our personal
relationship with water

our need of it our joy of it —

Now it cuts like a razor
through my throat!

7/12

BACK GARDEN BIRDBATH

It seems there are sparrows who
also have to put one

toe in the water to test it
and wait then poke their

little beaks in then another test then
edge down in slowly then

have a regular quivering shake and
shiver right down in the

water with water beads flying in circles
then hop about then

fly right out

7/12

TALK

Talk to your body
talk to your soul

Talk to the thunder on the hill

Talk to God's world in
which we dwell

the day in tumult
the night that's still

Talk to creatures that
cross your path

lambs of peace
Tygers of wrath

The door that's shut
the door that's open

If we talk to God's world
we talk to God

Who's the only One Who
makes things happen

They say one went mad
talking to roses

but in their beauty
saw God's responses

The sunset pouring its
gold in the sky

filled his heart
as it filled his eye

and as he talked to the
air around him

The Friend found him

7/13

COMFORTING ME

My mother's comforting me with
1940s songs I grew up with

in our little post-war house in Oakland

I woke up this morning with this one
humming in my head

*"Kiss me once and kiss me twice and kiss me once again
it's been a long long time…"*

A couple of days now
I hear them wafting through

from where she is
her presence felt

me sick
she gone

to where I hope she's
safe and sound

7/14

HIGH-FLYING WIND

> *The world is but a road*
> *heaven a roadside inn*
> *true lovers leave them behind*
> *to reach the Beloved*
>   — Abu Said

There's definitely a high-flying
wind above this world

and a bridge of crystal light that
connects this world with the

next

You can hear the impatient stamping of
hooves of centaurs *buraq*s and

gryphons on its planks as the whistling air
rushes past their ears

There's a bluish-white cloud that
unrotates its innermost whorl

sending out voices
calling us one by one

I think of them as I strain to
hear them in the straits of my distress

The Entity beyond entities

calling to us

from His indissoluble place

There's a sky above the
sky of this world where

this takes place

Have we been there before that we
know the sound of its voice?

Do we carry with us the
marks of having known that place?

I want to merge with it
out of my skin

my bone ladder of duration
holding me in

There's a river of light
flowing above this world

as well as the next

where golden boats
row toward His

Indescribable Face

Though crowded with

rowers there's always
one empty place

>   7/21

---

buraq: The wingéd human-faced horse or donkey that took
the Prophet, *salla 'llahu alayhi wa sallam*, on his Ascension

MY THROAT

I wake up to another day with
a knife at my throat

and it's my *throat!*

7/21

PALPABLE HUGS

If I sat still long enough
would the world slow down to a

hum?

Would tyrants slide off it
into the dark?

Would angels embrace everyone with
palpable hugs?

Their silken wings surrounding us
like the wings of translucent bugs?

Hunched over a golden breeze
I hear my shrunken stomach

slightly lurch
unable to face lunch

The animals of the world are
surprised to see me thin

gaunt eyes looking out from
my usual face

It's not the end of the line
but I can hear the train bell

toll a regular beat

It's OK
Its ring is sweet

									7/21

PHOENIX

Out my prison window I can
watch the fabulous birds

landscapes melting into each other
bridges going up into clouds

how the sky changes from
mauve to black and

back again
as the birds display their

courtship colors of
every known collapsing civilization

trembling in space

The prison walls are
my own skin

and how I've hemmed myself in here
by my own stitching

and how I'm here to unstitch my hem
unstitch by unstitch

until the walls fall away
and the phoenix I see

flaming into being from a far fountain
is the soul propelled to

certainty and a
station of unchanging light

facing God direct

I knock at my own prison door
to let me out

and that God alone
vouchsafe me

the key

7/22

RAINBOW PUDDLES

A rainbow came in and sat
down and said

*"It's not easy being the
revealed aspect of light"*

to which I nodded in sympathy

and to demonstrate
it stretched out between two

canyons the room we were in
accommodating itself to this

implacable display

this time with water drops falling and
each one of them miniature

aquariums of refracted beams
hovering over the pair of abysses

a glorious sight that
swept into its embrace wheeling

condors and a few rainbow-splattered eagles

in this incessant circumferential hunt
circling and circling the

equally wheeling sky
like searchlights finding

the hidden Face of God
cloud shapes catching sprays of

ignited sparks from that immensity
and turning them

back to water
falling in rainbow puddles

at our feet

7/26

THE WORLD

I don't know anymore where the world is
just as our fingertips touch a

cold pane of glass

having skimmed so many thousand
delicious surfaces

each one moving away from us
as we think they approach ever

closer but swim past us
into that cutout landscape

always around us
speaking or silent

animate or dead to the world themselves
the sure clue to our escape

as it withdraws from us or
we withdraw into a

cooler room
where dervishes turn

slowly in the dark to an
innermost music

7/28

MORPHO BLUE

The snowfall of summer is the
heat that expands the air

Where does fire's red come from
if not the sun?

All earth's oceans reflect every
star in space

Our star's twinkle depends
on the light of its soul

If we all stood as tall as we could
would we see over the
edges of space?

If we saw clearly into the
next world would it
deflect our actions in this?

Every good thought is an
angel bursting from a
womb of light

When someone leaves this world
it's like they've
stepped off a curb
into the wind

The perfection of the way things have been made
is its own proof by the
way things are

This world is all soft focus
the next world sharp

The marvelous never ceases to amaze
but the heart must have
amazed eyes to see it

A constant stream of creatures
lifts off into the skies
some with wings some not

The doors we see on earth
are nothing compared to the

doors in Paradise
all opening to a different music

Pure light comes to us at a
flick of our inner switch

Allah envelopes without enveloping
when we recognize the

pervasiveness of His Seeing
and we are like butterflies in

cocoons given fabulous
colors by His Sight

Morpho Blue just
one of its iridescences

In the middle of the night
the breath of nearness
is most near

Redemption happens the way
water falls

Forgiveness is air
let into an airless room

Even at the top of the highest peak
we can't just step off into the sky

At some point only God's Love has
any reality

and everything hangs enraptured from that
ferocious hook

Streams of light continue to
enter us from we
know not where

The truth of our beings —
light streaming everywhere

8/3

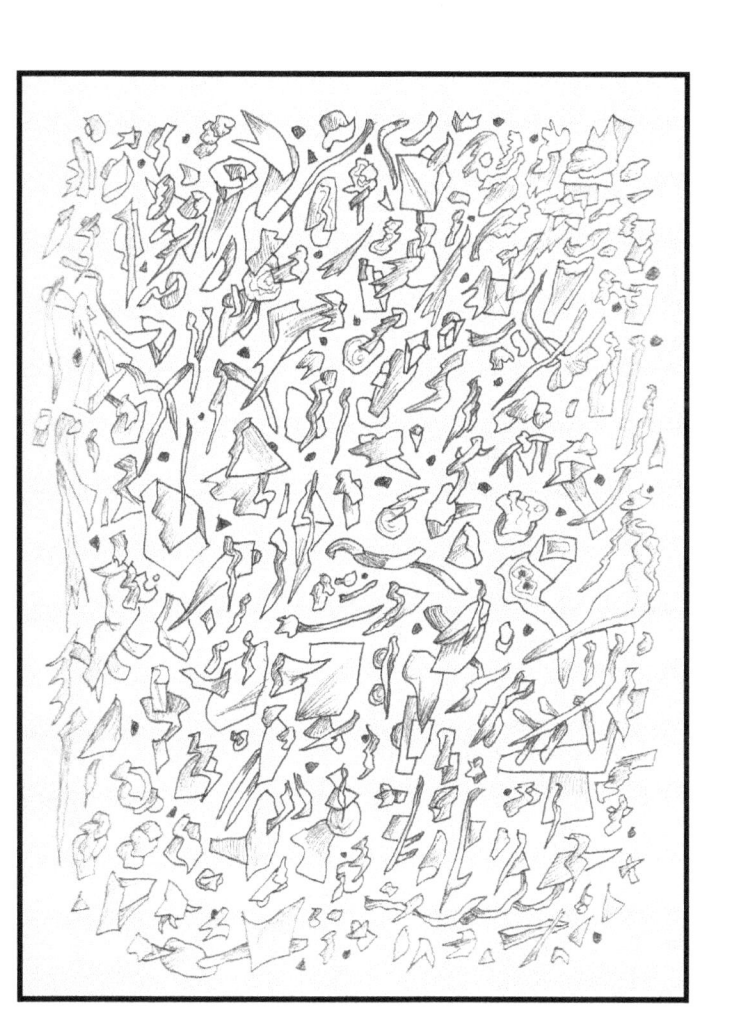

INDEX

A Little Blue Monk   60
A Rage of Bravery   105
Acceptable   89
All Moving Forward in Time   22
All Our Attempts at Healing   115
Allah   51
All's Well   49
Angelic Shoes   13
Back Garden Birdbath   141
Cancer   86
Comforting Me   144
Dark Chemo Thoughts   103
Ever-Ocean-Flowing Space   113
Faithful Slippers   138
Falling   58
God of the Splinter   11
Good Cheer Among the Cynics   15
High-Flying Wind   146
His Most Precious Concern   111
How Many Sirens More   73
I Enter a Huge Temple   53
I Hear Nearby   44
If I Should Die Tonight   36
In the Dark Casino   118
Job Sits in His Chair   56
Last and First Words   30
Leaning My Head on my Hand   100
Morpho Blue   158
My Mother   32
My Throat   149
Newspaper Fantasy   107
One Voice Calling Us   93

Only One Thing   106
On the Sheer Sides of Things   123
Our Hurts   121
Palpable Hugs   150
Phoenix   152
Poem Begun With a Line by Thomas Tranströmer   39
Poem Ending with Lines by Yeats   47
Prayer   29
Rainbow Puddles   155
Science Fact Science Fiction   43
Seeing the Scaffold   19
Short Fable of the Three Schooners   17
Small Town   70
Soul Questions   74
Sweat and Boils   25
Talk   142
The Bloom Upon the Rose   120
The Body   94
The Chemo   52
The Finite Sing of the Infinite?   130
The First Two Lines Came During Radiation # 7   72
The Lions' Arena   41
The Night is a Red Jacket   136
The Rowers   63
The Soul   67
The World   157
Twenty-Eight Poems Ago   133
Velvets and Icy Metals   125
Venetian Magicians   27
Water   140
What Fire Prevented   78
Wisdom   91
Written in Parking Lot after Radiation   109
Young Picadilly People   128

ABOUT THE AUTHOR

Born in 1940 in Oakland, California, Daniel Abdal-Hayy Moore had his first book of poems, *Dawn Visions*, published by Lawrence Ferlinghetti of City Lights Books, San Francisco, in 1964, and the second in 1972, *Burnt Heart/Ode to the War Dead*. He created and directed *The Floating Lotus Magic Opera Company* in Berkeley, California in the late 60s, and presented two major productions, *The Walls Are Running Blood*, and *Bliss Apocalypse*. He became a Sufi Muslim in 1970, performed the Hajj in 1972, and lived and traveled throughout Morocco, Spain, Algeria and Nigeria, landing in California and publishing *The Desert is the Only Way Out*, and *Chronicles of Akhira* in the early 80s (Zilzal Press). Residing in Philadelphia since 1990, in 1996 he published *The Ramadan Sonnets* (Jusoor/City Lights), and in 2002, *The Blind Beekeeper* (Jusoor/Syracuse University Press). He has been poetry editor for Seasons Journal and Islamica Magazine, and the major editor for a number of books, including *The Burdah* of Shaykh Busiri, and *The Prayer of the Oppressed* of Imam Nasir al-Dar'i, translated by Shaykh Hamza Yusuf, and the poetry of Palestinian poet, Mahmoud Darwish, translated by Munir Akash, including *Adam of Two Edens, State of Siege*, from Jusoor/Syracuse University Press, and *Unfortunately it was Paradise*, from the University of California Press. He is also widely published on the worldwide web: The American Muslim, and his own blog: www.ecstaticxchange.wordpress.com, and his website: www.danielmoorepoetry.com, among others. He has been a winner of the Nazim Hikmet Poetry Prize, for 2011 and 2012. The Ecstatic Exchange Series is bringing out the extensive body of his works of poetry (the full list of the books in print on facing page).

other books by the author

POETRY
Dawn Visions
Burnt Heart/Ode to the War Dead
This Body of Black Light Gone Through the Diamond
The Desert is the Only Way Out
The Chronicles of Akhira
The Blind Beekeeper
Mars & Beyond
Laughing Buddha Weeping Sufi
Salt Prayers
Ramadan Sonnets
Psalms for the Brokenhearted
I Imagine a Lion
Coattails of the Saint
Abdallah Jones and the Disappearing-Dust Caper (illustrated by the author)
Love is a Letter Burning in a High Wind
The Flame of Transformation Turns to Light
Underwater Galaxies
The Music Space
Cooked Oranges
Through Rose Colored Glasses
Like When You Wave at a Train and the Train Hoots Back at You
In the Realm of Neither
The Fire Eater's Lunchbreak
Millennial Prognostications
You Open a Door and it's a Starry Night
Where Death Goes
Shaking the Quicksilver Pool
The Perfect Orchestra
Sparrow on the Prophet's Tomb
A Maddening Disregard for the Passage of Time
Stretched Out on Amethysts
Invention of the Wheel
Sparks Off the Main Strike
Chants for the Beauty Feast
In Constant Incandescence
Holiday from the Perfect Crime
The Caged Bear Spies the Angel
The Puzzle
Ramadan is Burnished Sunlight
Ala-udeen & The Magic Lamp (illustrated by the author)
The Crown of Creation (illustrated by the author)
Blood Songs
Down at the Deep End (with drawings by the author)

THEATER / THE FLOATING LOTUS MAGIC OPERA COMPANY
The Walls Are Running Blood
Bliss Apocalypse

PROSE
Zen Rock Gardening
The Little Book of Zen

POETIC WORKS by Daniel Abdal-Hayy Moore
Published and Unpublished

Dawn Visions (published by City Lights, 1964)
Burnt Heart/Ode to the War Dead (published by City Lights, 1972)
This Body of Black Light Gone Through the Diamond (printed by Fred Stone, Cambridge, Mass, 1965)
On The Streets at Night Alone (1965?)
All Hail the Surgical Lamp (1967)
States of Amazement (1970)

Abdallah Jones and the Disappearing-Dust Caper (published by The Ecstatic Exchange/Crescent Series, 2006)
Ala-udeen and the Magic Lamp (published by The Ecstatic Exchange/Crescent Series, 2011)
The Chronicles of Akhira (1981) (published by Zilzal Press with Typoglyphs by Karl Kempton, 1986) (published in Sparrow on the Prophet's Tomb, The Ecstatic Exchange, 2010)
Mouloud (1984) (A Zilzal Press chapbook, 1995) (published in Sparrow on the Prophet's Tomb, The Ecstatic Exchange, 2010)
The Crown of Creation (1984)(published by The Ecstatic Exchange, 2012)
The Look of the Lion (The Parabolas of Sight) (1984)
The Desert is the Only Way Out (completed 4/21/84) (Zilzal Press chapbook, 1985)
Atomic Dance (1984) (am here books, 1988)
Outlandish Tales (1984)
Awake as Never Before (12/26/84) (Zilzal Press chapbook, 1993)
Glorious Intervals (1/1/85) (Zilzal Press chapbook, ?)
Long Days on Earth/Book I (1/28 – 8/30/85)
Long Days on Earth/Book II (Hayy Ibn Yaqzan)
Long Days on Earth/Book III (1/22/86)
Long Days on Earth/Book IV (1986)
The Ramadan Sonnets (Long Days on Earth/Book V) (5/9 – 6/11/86) (published by Jusoor/City Lights Books, 1996) (republished as Ramadan Sonnets by The Ecstatic Exchange, 2005)
Long Days on Earth/Book VI (6-8/30/86)
Holograms (9/4/86 – 3/26/87)

History of the World (The Epic of Man's Survival) (4/7 – 6/18/87)
Exploratory Odes (6/25 – 10/18/87)
The Man at the End of the World (11/11 – 12/10/87)
The Perfect Orchestra (3/30 – 7/25/88)
Fed from Underground Springs (7/30 – 11/23/88)
Ideas of the Heart (11/27/88 – 5/5/89)
New Poems (scattered poems, out of series, from 3/24 – 8/9/89)
Facing Mecca (5/16 – 11/11/89)
A Maddening Disregard for the Passage of Time (11/17/89 – 5/20/90)
The Heart Falls in Love with Visions of Perfection (6/15/90 – 6/2/91)
Like When You Wave at a Train and the Train Hoots Back at You (Farid's Book) (6/11 – 7/26/91) (published by The Ecstatic Exchange, 2008)
Orpheus Meets Morpheus (8/1/91– 3/14/92)
The Puzzle (3/21/92 – 8/17/93) (published by The Ecstatic Exchange, 2011)
The Greater Vehicle (10/17/93 – 4/30/94)
A Hundred Little 3-D Pictures (5/14/94 – 9/11/95)
The Angel Broadcast (9/29 – 12/17/95)
Mecca/Medina Time-Warp (12/19/95 – 1/6/96) (published as a Zilzal Press chapbook, 1996) (Published in Sparrow on the Prophet's Tomb, The Ecstatic Exchange, 2010)
Miracle Songs for the Millennium (1/20 – 10/16/96)
The Blind Beekeeper (11/15/96 – 5/30/97) (published 2002 by Jusoor/Syracuse University Press)
Chants for the Beauty Feast (6/3 – 10/28/97) (published by The Ecstatic Exchange, 2011)
You Open a Door and it's a Starry Night (10/29/97 – 5/23/98) (published by The Ecstatic Exchange, 2009)
Salt Prayers (5/29 – 10/24/98) (published by The Ecstatic Exchange, 2005)
Some (10/25/98 – 4/25/99)
Flight to Egypt (5/1 – 5/16/99)
I Imagine a Lion (5/21 – 11/15/99) (published by The Ecstatic Exchange, 2006)
Millennial Prognostications (11/25/99 – 2/2/2000) (published by the Ecstatic Exchange, 2009)
Shaking the Quicksilver Pool (2/4 – 10/8/2000) (Published by The Ecstatic Exchange, 2009)
Blood Songs (10/9/2000 – 4/3/2001) (Published by The Ecstatic Exchange, 2012)
The Music Space (4/10 – 9/16/2001) (Published by The Ecstatic Exchange, 2007)
Where Death Goes (9/20/2001 – 5/1/2002) (Published by The Ecstatic Exchange, 2009)

The Flame of Transformation Turns to Light (99 Ghazals Written in English) (5/14 – 8/21/2002) (Published by The Ecstatic Exchange, 2007)
Through Rose-Colored Glasses (7/22/2002 – 1/15/2003) (Published by The Ecstatic Exchange, 2007)
Psalms for the Broken-Hearted (1/22 – 5/25/2003) (Published by The Ecstatic Exchange, 2006)
Hoopoe's Argument (5/27 – 9/18/03)
Love is a Letter Burning in a High Wind (9/21 – 11/6/2003) (Published by The Ecstatic Exchange, 2006)
Laughing Buddha/Weeping Sufi (11/7/2003 – 1/10/2004) (Published by The Ecstatic Exchange, 2005)
Mars and Beyond (1/20 – 3/29/2004) (Published by The Ecstatic Exchange, 2005)
Underwater Galaxies (4/5 – 7/21/2004) (Published by The Ecstatic Exchange, 2007)
Cooked Oranges (7/23/2004 – 1/24/2005) (Published by The Ecstatic Exchange, 2007)
Holiday from the Perfect Crime (1/25 – 6/11/2005) (published by The Ecstatic Exchange, 2011)
Stories Too Fiery to Sing Too Watery to Whisper (6/13 – 10/24/2005)
Coattails of the Saint (10/26/2005 – 5/10/2006) (Published by The Ecstatic Exchange, 2006)
In the Realm of Neither (5/14/2006 – 11/12/06) (Published by The Ecstatic Exchange, 2008)
Invention of the Wheel (11/13/06 – 6/10/07) (Published by The Ecstatic Exchange, 2010)
The Sound of Geese Over the House (6/15 – 11/4/07)
The Fire Eater's Lunchbreak (11/11/07 – 5/19/2008) (Published by The Ecstatic Exchange, 2008)
Sparks Off the Main Strike (5/24/2008 – 1/10/2009) (published by The Ecstatic Exchange, 2010)
Stretched Out on Amethysts (1/13 – 9/17/2009) (published by The Ecstatic Exchange, 2010)
The Throne Perpendicular to All that is Horizontal (9/18/09 – 1/25/10)
In Constant Incandescence (2/10 – 8/13/10) (published by The Ecstatic Exchange, 2011)
The Caged Bear Spies the Angel (8/30/10 –3/6/11)(published by The Ecstatic Exchange, 2011)
This Light Slants Upward (3/7/11 – 10/13/11)
Ramadan is Burnished Sunlight (part of This Light Slants Upward, published separately by The Ecstatic Exchange, 2011)

The Match That Becomes a Conflagration (10/14/11 – 5/9/12)
Down at the Deep End (5/10 – 8/3/12) (published by The Ecstatic Exchange, 2012)
Next Life (8/9/12 –)